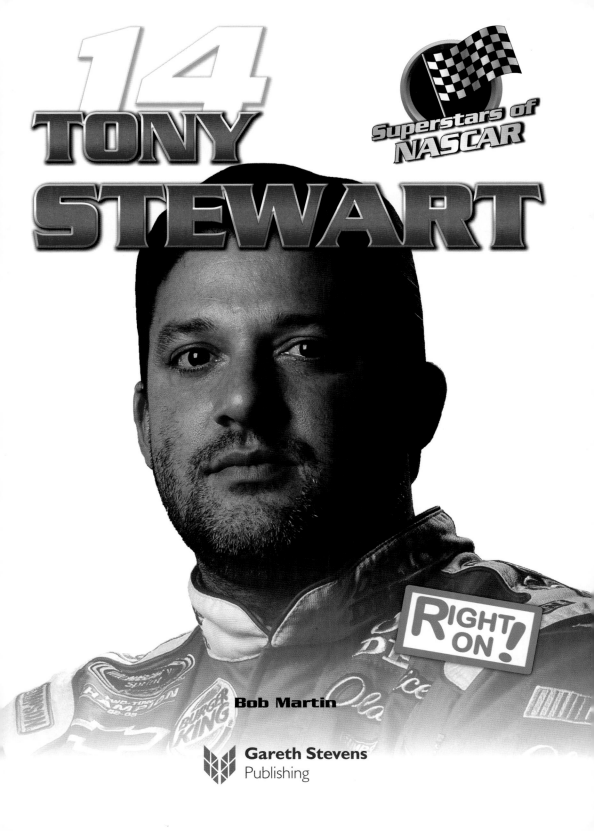

Please visit our Web site, www.garethstevens.com. For a free color catalog of all our high-quality books, call toll free 1-800-542-2595 or fax 1-877-542-2596.

Library of Congress Cataloging-in-Publication Data

Martin, Bob.
Tony Stewart / Bob Martin.
    p. cm. — (Superstars of NASCAR)
Includes index.
ISBN 978-1-4339-3969-3 (pbk.)
ISBN 978-1-4339-3970-9 (6-pack)
ISBN 978-1-4339-3968-6 (library binding)
1. Stewart, Tony, 1971—Juvenile literature. 2. Automobile racing drivers—United States—Biography—Juvenile literature. I. Title.
GV1032.S743M37 2010
796.72092—dc22
[B]
                                        2010007388

First Edition

Published in 2011 by
Gareth Stevens Publishing
111 East 14th Street, Suite 349
New York, NY 10003

Designer: Michael J. Flynn
Editor: Mary Ann Hoffman

Photo credits: Cover (Tony Stewart), pp. 1, 19, 25 Rusty Jarrett/Getty Images; cover, pp. 4, 6, 8, 10, 12, 14, 18, 20, 24, 26, 28 (background on all) Shutterstock.com; p. 5 Geoff Burke/Getty Images; p. 7 Racing Photo Archives/Getty Images; pp. 9, 11, 13 David Taylor/Getty Images; p. 15 RacingOne/ISC Archives/Getty Images; pp. 16–17 Darren Carroll/Sports Illustrated/Getty Images; p. 21 George Tiedemann/Sports Illustrated/Getty Images; pp. 22–23 Chris Graythen/Getty Images; p. 27 Elsa/Getty Images; p. 29 Jerry Markland/Getty Images.

Printed in the United States of America

CPSIA compliance information: Batch #CS10GS: For further information contact Gareth Stevens, New York, New York at 1-800-542-2595.

Contents

NASCAR Driver and Owner

Anthony Wayne "Tony" Stewart was born in Indiana on May 20, 1971. He is a famous NASCAR driver. He also owns a NASCAR racing team.

An Early Start

Tony Stewart started racing go-karts when he was about 7 years old. At the age of 16, he won the World Karting Championship.

At the age of 24, Tony was the first driver to win the USAC "Triple Crown." In one season, he won three championships racing different types of cars on paved and dirt tracks.

9

Indy Cars

Tony moved up to Indy cars after winning the Triple Crown. Indy cars are single-seat, open-wheeled cars. In 1997, Tony was the Indy Racing League winner.

Tony Stewart

11

NASCAR

Tony also began racing stock cars in NASCAR. Stock cars look like regular cars.

13

In 1999, Tony was named Rookie of the Year in the Winston Cup Series—the leading NASCAR racing series. It is now called the Sprint Cup Series.

Tony Stewart

Championships

In 2002, Tony won the top level NASCAR championship. He won it again in 2005!

Helping Others

Tony formed Tony Stewart Racing (TSR) in 2000. TSR runs four sprint car teams that have won several championships. It also hires and trains young racers.

The Tony Stewart Foundation was formed in 2003. It raises money to help children, animals, and people hurt in motorsports.

A Speedway Owner

Tony bought a racetrack called Eldora Speedway in 2004. It was built in 1954. Many special races are held at this dirt track.

A 2006 race at Eldora Speedway did not take place because of rain. Tony won the makeup race. He was so happy that he jumped over the fence into the crowd!

25

A Team of His Own

In 2008, Tony decided to leave his racing team of many years. He became an owner of Stewart-Haas Racing. He also became a driver for the team.

Tony Stewart has won many races in sprint cars, Indy cars, and stock cars. He loves to race. He loves to win!

Timeline

1971 Tony is born in Indiana.

1995 Tony wins the USAC "Triple Crown."

1997 Tony wins the Indy Racing League championship.

1999 Tony is named Rookie of the Year in the top NASCAR series.

2000 Tony forms Tony Stewart Racing.

2002 Tony wins his first top level NASCAR championship.

2003 Tony starts the Tony Stewart Foundation.

2004 Tony buys Eldora Speedway.

2008 Tony becomes an owner of Stewart-Haas Racing.

For More Information

Books:

Basen, Ryan. *Tony Stewart: Rocket on the Racetrack.* Berkeley Heights, NJ: Enslow Publishers, 2008.

Teitelbaum, Michael. *Tony Stewart.* Mankato, MN: Child's World, 2009.

Web Sites:

How NASCAR Race Cars Work
auto.howstuffworks.com/auto-racing/nascar/nascar-basics/nascar.htm

Tony Stewart
www.tonystewart.azplayers.com

Publisher's note to educators and parents: Our editors have carefully reviewed these Web sites to ensure that they are suitable for students. Many Web sites change frequently, however, and we cannot guarantee that a site's future contents will continue to meet our high standards of quality and educational value. Be advised that students should be closely supervised whenever they access the Internet.

Glossary

championship: a series of races to decide a winner

foundation: an organization that raises money

go-kart: a small racing car

motorsports: racing and other sports done with cars and motorcycles

rookie: a person in their first year of a sport

sprint car: small, high-powered race cars that race on dirt or paved tracks

USAC: United States Auto Club

Index